Carving Clowns

by
Jim Maxwell

Fox Chapel Publishing Co Inc.

Box 7948
Lancaster, Pennsylvania
17604

© 1996 by Fox Chapel Publishing

Publisher: Alan Giagnocavo
Project Editor: Ayleen Stellhorn
Electronic Specialist: Bob Altland, Altland Design
Cover and Gallery Photography: Bob Polett, VMI Communications
Step-by-Step Photography: Jim and Margie Maxwell
Back Cover Photo: Jim Baer
ISBN # 1–56523–060–4
Printed in Hong Kong

To order your copy of this book,
please send check or money order
for cover price plus $2.50 to:
Fox Chapel Book Orders
Box 7948
Lancaster, PA 17604–7948

Try your favorite book supplier first!

Table of Contents

Foreword

There are many different styles and personalities of clowns, all of which originally derived from three basic kinds of clowns—the White Face, the Auguste, and the Black Face. As a young boy, I enjoyed watching the performances of all kinds of clowns. As a carver, I still enjoy watching clowns perform, but I find that clowns are a wonderful subject to carve.

The crazy antics of the real clowns, such as dancing, juggling, falling down or doing acrobatics, provide me with plenty of ideas for putting a lot of action into my carved clowns. However, I think the strongest thing that has attracted my interest is the many unique expressions used by real clowns when they paint their faces. These combined elements, plus their wide assortment of colorful costumes, has made clown carving one of my favorite subjects.

I now invite you to join me in the pages of this book as we create and carve clowns from the past, present and future. I have included 12 of my favorite clown patterns plus detailed step-by-step instructions for carving and painting clowns. By the time we are finished, I am sure your interest and appreciation for clowns and clowning will have grown considerably, plus we will have shared the experience of some very enjoyable and fun-filled wood carving.

Happy Carving
Jim Maxwell
Maxwell's Wood Carving
Cole Camp, Missouri

How To Use This Book

The first eight clown patterns in this book have been arranged to coincide with their appropriate place in the history of clowning and not necessarily according to their degree of carving difficulty.

I have included detailed step-by-step photos for two of the clowns—the White Face and the Black Face. You can use these instructions to help you carve the remaining clowns in this book. In addition, I have also included blocking instructions for Yankee Dan and the Auguste Clown, as blocking these two figures is quite complicated. Painting instructions are included in the color section toward the back of the book. Color photos of each of the clowns are included in the color section entitled Clowns on Parade.

When following the carving steps for these projects, you will want to rotate your work often to ensure that you are carving a balanced figure. Some photos were taken from the best camera advantage, and you may find that you'll have to hold the carving or your tool in a different manner. Remember, it is not necessary to duplicate every one of my cuts in the order that I present them. You may find a different way to get the same results.

I carve mostly with a knife to achieve a clean, smooth style that I have used for years. While many instructors use gouges to create a rough-cut look, which works well on many caricatures, it is not my preferred way of carving. You, however, may wish to try different cuts to vary the look of your finished clowns.

If you are a beginning carver, you'll want to study the first few pages of this book carefully. They include important information about safety, sharpening tools, choosing patterns and selecting wood. Of course, this book is not designed to teach a novice how to carve. My goal is to introduce you to carving clowns and provide you with patterns and step-by-step instructions to get you started.

With these points in mind, let's begin.

Safety First

I hope this book and the projects enclosed will provide many fun-filled and accident free hours of enjoyment for fellow carvers. However, carving clowns does not mean we will clown around with safety.

Before we even pick up our tools, I would like to pass on to you a few safety tips that I have learned through years of experience.

#1 Sharp Tools

Sharp tools are the safest tools. Dull tools slip and cut fingers. So, for your benefit I have enclosed a full chapter on sharpening dedicated to solving this problem.

#2 Protective Gloves

Wear some protection on your hands. If you carve with a knife, wear a leather thumb guard on the hand that holds the knife. When carving with gouges and v-tools, wear a wood carver's mesh glove. These high-tech bullet proof gloves resist most cuts and are well worth the price. When carving with the gouges and v-tools, be very careful to never place the hand holding the wood in the direct path of the cutting tool.

#3 Controlled Cuts with a Knife

I believe the safest way to remove wood is shown in the third photo of the chapter on the White Face Clown (page 21). In this photo, I am placing my right thumb on the project and pulling the knife across the wood toward the thumb as if I were peeling a potato. It is important to note that two small cuts are just as effective as one large one and a whole lot safer.

#4 Controlled Cuts with V-tools and Gouges

When using the small v-tools or gouges, I usually hold the tool in the palm of my right hand and place my right thumb firmly on the project. A slight movement of the wrist will move the tool a safe, controllable distance (photo #83, page 34).

#5 Carving Small Features

When carving items such as thumbs, fingers and noses, it is best to start the cut at the smallest or weakest point and apply pressure toward the larger, or stronger part, when possible. This will reduce breakage and prevent a lot of cut fingers.

#6 Carve Within Your Skill Level

It is best to choose projects that are in your skill level. Although complicated designs are impressive, they require greater maneuvering of the tools and sometimes the project must be held in an awkward position. Your hands should be strong enough to hold the project securely and still be able to apply enough pressure to safely make the cuts.

#7 Vises

When using larger tools and removing large chips of wood, I suggest clamping the project in a vise or to the work bench, but be careful. As the project progresses and becomes rounded, it becomes more and more difficult to hold it securely in a vise and the powerful jaws of a vise can crush or mar a delicate piece. Most of the time I use large screws to attach a hexagon block of wood to the bottom of my projects. Then I clamp this block in the vise as tightly as I needed. I can then apply greater amounts of pressure when carving and use a mallet, if necessary, without worrying about damaging my carving or having the carving slip. The longer or larger tools should be held by the handle with the right hand. Guide the tool's cutting edge with the left hand (assuming you are right-handed).

#8 Band Saws

When bandsawing the figures, keep the blade sharp, the safety guards properly set, and keep thumbs and fingers out of the direct path of the blade. Make sure the material being cut lays completely flat on the saw table. As I saw out the side view of my figure, I often use paper masking tape to tape the pieces of scrap back on my projects.

Safety First

The paper masking tape will not dull the blade and by doing this I can turn the project over and cut the front view without the figure tipping or rocking on the saw table.

#9 POWER TOOLS

If you use a power carver for quick removal of excess wood on your projects, then you should definitely read all of the manufacturer's operating instructions and become familiar with the safety procedures for using such tools before you begin.

#10 COMMON SENSE

Safety for the most part is just good common sense. So take your time, relax and think about what you are doing. Follow these safety tips and you will have a safe and enjoyable hobby.

#11 PAINTS

The acrylic water-based paint that Margie uses on the carvings poses no serious health problems, as far as we know. Of course, it is always a good habit to paint in an area with proper ventilation. This measure is necessary with other paints that may have stronger, and sometimes very dangerous, fumes.

#12 ANTIQUING FINISHES

The two ingredients Margie uses for the antique finish are linseed oil and burnt umber oil color. This mixture, because of the linseed oil, is spontaneously combustible and very dangerous. All wiping rags and paper towels should be disposed of properly. Be sure to place them in a fruit jar or other such air tight container immediately after use. Never place such materials in a trash can or trash bag unless they are first sealed in an air tight container.

Tools & Sharpening

Before you begin carving, you will need a few of the things found in my tool box. First and most important is a good straight-blade carving knife. I also have a small $1/8$ inch drill bit with a fixed handle, a small round file for making tiny holes through the clowns hands, a small awl and a pair of calipers for measuring. For the more advanced figures in this book we will be using a few wood carving tools.

My favorite tools (pictured at right) are: a 3mm v-tool, an 8mm v-tool, a 1mm deep gouge, a 2mm deep gouge, a 4mm deep gouge, a 5mm medium gouge, a 5mm shallow gouge, an 8mm shallow gouge and a 12mm shallow gouge.

If your tools are like mine, then chances are they will probably need to be sharpened before you begin carving. For this task you will need a soft Arkansas stone, honing oil and a leather strop.

I believe that sharpening is probably more difficult to learn than carving. But to learn to carve, you must have sharp tools, and to have sharp tools you must learn some sharpening techniques.

I've outlined some of the steps for sharpening knives, gouges and v-tools below.

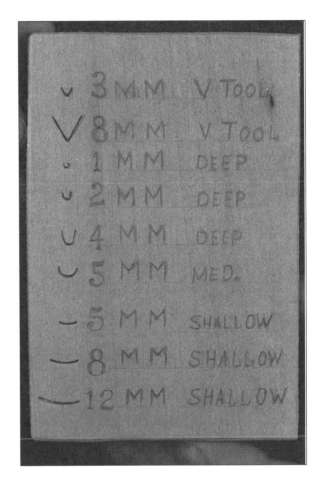

To sharpen a knife, lay the knife flat on the oiled stone, then raise the back of the blade slightly (about 18 degrees). Rotate the knife in a circular motion as shown in the photo. Turn the knife over and repeat these steps. Stone both sides of the blade until the edge becomes thin and sharp.

Next, strop the blade to remove any burrs or roughness left by the stone. You can make a strop by gluing a piece of leather to a thin piece of wood. Coat the leather with a white buffing rouge. I make one end of my strop very thin so it will fit inside the small gouges and v-tools.

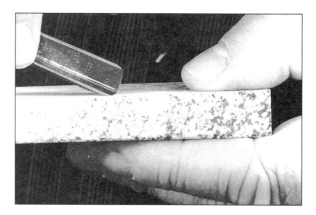

To sharpen a gouge, place the bevel flat on the oiled stone. Press lightly on the cutting edge and rotate the tool in a circular motion. Turn the tool slightly from side to side as you work to ensure uniform sharpness. Strop the gouge by pulling it backwards over the strop.

Sharpening a v-tool is a bit more tricky. I usually place the right side bevel on the stone first and sharpen it with a circular motion.

Then I sharpen the left side bevel by repeating the same process on the left side.

In this photo I am sharpening the point or bottom of the v tool to match the inside contour of the tool. Look closely at the photo showing tool sizes on page 3, and you can see the v-tool is rounded at the bottom, where the two sides join together. Sharpen this area as if it were the bottom of a 1mm deep gouge. Be careful not to remove too much metal or you will end up with a tiny notch where the two sides join together. Strop the outer sides of the v-tool by pulling the tool backward over the strop.

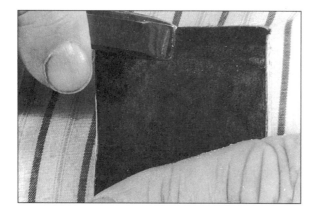

You must also strop the inside of a v-tool or a gouge by placing it over the thin edge of the strop and pulling it backwards. Never use rough stones on the inside of a gouge and v-tool. This area should be polished with a strop only.

Choosing and Altering Patterns

The first step of tackling any project is creating the necessary interest and inspiration to put one's energy and skills to work long enough to accomplish the desired task. For me this means setting the right mood and becoming familiar with the subject I wish to create. This often requires a great deal of time and research and exposure to items or artifacts pertaining to my chosen subject.

In order to meet the challenge of creating 12 different clown patterns for this book, I began by buying a couple of tickets and attending a three ring circus with my wife Margie just to watch the clowns perform. The following day during a trip to the library, we found many books on the circus and clowning. The next few evenings found me searching through my old antique toy magazines, which provided several photos of old toy clowns. While digging through my toy collection, I was able to find two antique tin toy clowns and some old circus posters of clowns. These are all events or subject matter which have contributed to the patterns in this book. Creating a new and original pattern is sometimes the most enjoyable part of the project for me.

Before you select a pattern in this book, consider your own skill level. Are you a beginning carver or a more experienced carver? If you are a beginning carver, you'll want to start with the White Face Clown or the Black Face Clown. Advanced carvers may want to try their hand at the other figures in this book. Once you have carved some of the projects in this book and become familiar with clowns, you may want to try creating your own patterns.

You can start making new patterns by altering the patterns in this book. A fun challenge would be to take the Butterfly Catcher and change his butterfly net to a long pole with small wire animal snare or hoop on the end. Remove the back and sides of the hat brim to make his hat a cap, add the words ANIMAL CONTROL across the front of the crown, and presto, we now have a Dog Catcher Clown. Or try putting the realistic Auguste head on Margie's little ornament clown. Carve fingers and feet. This combination will give us a nice midget clown. Most clown features are traditional. It is the combinations of these old traditions plus the additions of new ideas that give us new and original clowns.

As I mentioned before, creating original patterns is an enjoyable challenge for the more experienced carver. Start with plenty of reference material and combine elements you find interesting. Be sure not to copy anyone else's design directly. An unwritten rule of clowning calls for each clown to develop his own act; carvers must also strive to be original.

Ten clowns are hidden in this photo. Take a minute to look carefully at the picture. Can you find all ten of the clowns?

Selecting Wood

Years ago when I first began carving, getting wood meant I had only to walk down the hill to my Father's sawmill and I had an unlimited supply of choice woods for carving. But since Dad has retired, I now must go to the lumber yard and buy my wood just as other carvers do. I prefer going to the larger lumber yards. They will usually have the basswood or butternut wood used for carving the characters. However, the mail-order speciality wood supplier is often the only source available to people in some locations. To learn the addresses and locations of wood dealers, I suggest joining the National Wood Carvers Association (see information in back pages), as they have a publication which regularly lists dealers and suppliers.

If you buy your wood at the lumber yard, you should purchase straight grain. The wood should be free of knots and white or tan in color. If two pieces of wood are the exact size and one feels lighter in weight, then the lighter weight piece will carve easier. When basswood ages, it shrinks and the grain becomes dense, thus making it heavier and harder to carve. Kiln-dried basswood is best. Very dark black streaks or spots found in some pieces of basswood are attributed to a variety of growing conditions. These spots will immediately dull a knife or tool and do not carve well.

Soft gray coloring and streaks are caused by moisture and mildew in the log after it has been cut and left laying in the log yard several days before sawing into lumber. This does not mean the wood can't be carved and often this gray coloration does not run too deep. However, it does show through thin paint colors on your finished projects, so avoid it when possible.

Photo #3 of the White Face Clown shows two small knots in the right leg. Photo #21 shows these same knots rounded and close-up. You should not allow knots any larger than this in your carving and certainly never in the head area.

Many pieces of basswood have hairline cracks in the ends of the material. I always throw away the first two or three inches of wood on each plank. These cracks can cause the carving to break and, in the process, seriously injure a carver.

If it is impossible for you to get basswood, then sugar pine or white ponderosa pine can be purchased at most small lumber yards. You can laminate the wood to get the desired thickness, but be absolutely sure you have sugar pine or ponderosa pine. Spruce, fir and yellow pine will not carve well, and most small lumber yards refer to all building materials as pine.

Most wood carving shows and carving shops provide both a variety of supplies and inspiration. Try to visit one.

Court Jester

THE COURT JESTER, SOMETIMES CALLED A JOKER, IS usually thought of as the first merry-maker of mirth, not yet called a clown, but certainly a professional laugh-maker. These jolly entertainers performed without facial make-up as they jested, danced and played music for the kings of the Middle Ages. My Court Jester pattern resembles the colorful Joker found in an ordinary deck of playing cards.

CARVING TIPS
If you wish to carve the Joker first and need some pointers on how to carve clowns, use the pattern for the Court Jester but follow the instructions for the White Face Clown.

The parade stick that the Jester is holding and the Jester's head were carved separately. To achieve the look of the tight fitting costume I used small, smooth, precise knife cuts. I often use this technique on small, finely detailed figures.

PAINTING NOTES
The Joker was painted in red, black and white with some gold trimming. All the colors were applied very thin.

As the renaissance period ended, the Jesters began performing in traveling minstrel shows and later in theaters. At this time, theaters in Europe were a form of entertainment only for heads of government and members of the aristocracy. Jesters were not permitted by the law to perform for the common people. To avoid recognition by law, the Jesters began painting their faces white and performing mute in the streets, thus creating the Pantomime or Mime performers.

Mime acts usually consisted of music, magic and agile body movements. Their acts always excluded the use of speech. Mime acting is still very popular today, so I have included a pattern for a modern day Mime to represent this form of entertainment.

Carving Tips

For basic instructions on how to carve the Mime, use the Mime pattern and refer to the steps outlined in the chapter about the White Face Clown. The only difference is that the Mime's head and body are sawed out as one piece, not two as in the case of the White Face Clown. Use small smooth cuts to assure a feminine look. All facial lines should be very smooth with a small nose.

Painting Notes

This female clown is wearing soft colors with white gloves and a very small amount of red and black facial make-up.

Carving Clowns

Black Face Clown
page 37

Black Face Clowns are always trying their best to get something done but failing miserably despite all their efforts. The three playful butterflies were carved separately and attached after the clown was finished.

White Face Clown
page 19

The White Face Clown is one of the earliest types of true clowns. They traditionally used red and black paint on their white faces and wore loose, brightly colored costumes. The two balls in the clown's hands were carved from the wood around the hands; the third was carved separately and suspended with a wire.

Mime
page 9

Mimes are silent clowns, but funny nonetheless. Their acts usually include music, magic tricks and acrobatics. This modern mime was carved from one piece of wood.

Court Jester
page 7

The Court Jester, also referred to as a joker, was making kings and queens laugh long before circus-type clowns became popular. To make this Court Jester's costume look like a tight-fitting body suit, the artist used small, precise knife cuts.

Clown of the Future
page 83

A creation of the artist's imagination, this little clown of the future flies a rocket ship and buzzes by laughing onlookers. The pattern for this clown was a combination of several ideas from the artist.

Parade Stick
page 79

Parade sticks were used as props by early clowns. This contemporary carving is a replica of an antique parade stick carved around the turn of the century.

Ornament Clown
page 8

Ornament clowns can be made from any pattern. Their miniature size, plus the addition of a string or other type of hanger, makes them ideal for use as Christmas ornaments.

Roly Poly Clown
page 77

This Roly Poly Clown is a replica of a 1910 White Face metal toy clown. Though the pattern for the clown looks simple, rounding the base can prove difficult.

Tramp Clown
page 75

Colorful patches and lapel flowers add a dash of color to this Tramp Clown's traditional dark-colored, well-worn clothing. Squinted eyes and a straight-forward head make this carving a good intermediate project.

Yankee Dan
page 37

Dan Rice was a famous clown during the late 1800s. His signature tall hat and red, white and blue outfit became the prototype for today's Uncle Sam. The position of the sign, the foot and the hands make this a difficult project to block out.

Rodeo Clown
page 65

Rodeo clowns have a funny appearance, but a serious job. These clowns use their antics to distract the attention of bucking broncos and wild bulls from their fallen riders. Concealing this clown's body in a barrel makes him an easy clown to carve.

Auguste Clown
page 41

At the turn of the century, these clowns, known as Auguste Clowns, began using a variety of colors on their faces and allowing colored hair to show through their skull caps. The drum, drumsticks and head for this piece were all carved separately.

White Face Clown

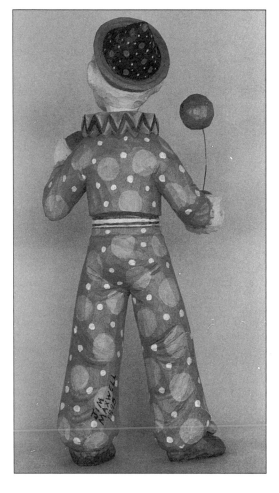

By the early part of the nineteenth century these white-faced performers were appearing in the European Circus. Now elite entertainers, they began using red and black paint on their white faces and wore loose-fitting, colorful costumes. The name clown had now been applied to the profession. Joseph Gremaldi, a clown of this time period (1781-1828) became so famous that every clown was now called a "joey" by people in the clown profession.

My White Face Clown will bear some resemblance to Joseph Gremaldi and also Harry Dann, a very famous modern day White Face Clown. I tried to make my figure as original as possible. A clown's character is his trade-mark. It is his exclusive property and although many real clowns appear similar in appearance, there is an unwritten law that clowns do not directly copy from one another.

Carving Tips
Step-by-step photos and detailed instruction for carving the White Face Clown follow. These basic instructions can also be used to help you carve other clowns.

Painting Notes
The colors used on the White Face Clown were a soft, yellow-green for the pants and jacket, with large yellow and small white polka dots. The shirt is white with dark green stripes. The collar and cuffs are trimmed in bright yellow. He has brown leather shoes with yellow fluffy tassels and his hat is two tones of green, with small yellow and white dots. Refer to the color photos when painting the clown's face.

To carve the White Face Clown you will need a choice piece of basswood 4" x 4" x 11". Trace the side view of the body and head on the wood and saw them out with a band saw. Make sure the grain of the wood is running vertically.

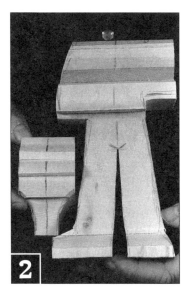

The next step is to draw the front view of the head and the body on your blank. Use calipers to check the waistline and collar. Be sure you have allowed enough wood around the right hand. Carefully bandsaw the front views. Draw a centerline around the head and body.

Begin removing wood from the upper chest. Be careful to leave the wood intact where the left hand will be located. You can also use a 10mm shallow gouge for this operation. If you opt to use a gouge, clamp the figure in a vise.

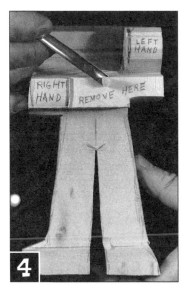

Next, mark the width of the right hand. Use a 10mm shallow gouge to remove excess wood from the center of the chest. Take care not to remove the wood that will form the right hand. This step can also be done while the figure is clamped in a vise.

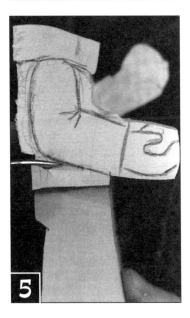

Once you have removed the wood from the chest, draw on the side view of the arms. Use a carving knife to remove wood from under the elbows. Repeat this process on both sides. Though this photo shows the figure in an upright position, this step can best be accomplished by holding the carving upside down.

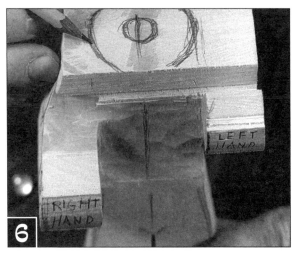

It is now time to turn your attention to the collar. To block out the collar, first draw on the top view.

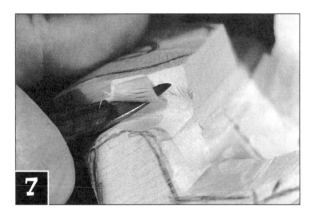

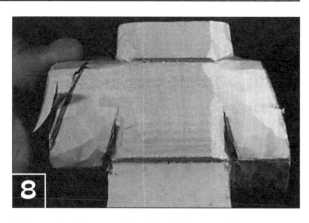

Block out the collar by removing wood from the top of the shoulders. Continue removing wood until you have reached the line you drew to mark the top view of the collar. Repeat this process on the opposite side.

This is a back view of the blocked-out collar. Use a carving knife to remove wood from this area to make the angle of the left arm match that of the right. Both shoulders should appear uniform from the back.

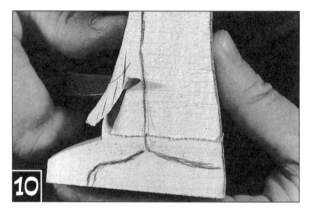

This upright photo shows the notch that has been carved under the elbows along the back. This step is easily accomplished by holding the carving upside down and using your carving knife.

The left leg is positioned farther back than the right leg, so you will need to remove the excess wood from in front of the left leg. To do this, draw on a side view of the left leg and, using a knife or gouge, remove the extra wood.

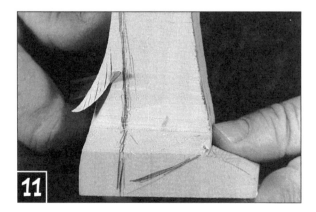

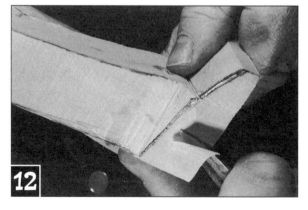

The right leg is in a slightly forward position with the toe pointing outward. Draw on a side view and remove the extra wood from behind the right leg. I like to use a knife for this step.

To narrow the heels, draw a line running from the heel to the toe on the outer side of the right foot. Remove this extra wood with your knife.

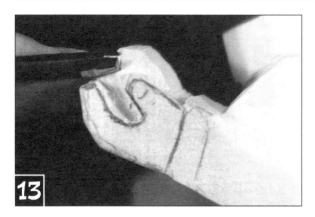

To block the hands, begin by drawing the side view of the left hand on the block. Use a 4mm deep gouge to remove wood from the outer side of the orange between the thumb and fingers.

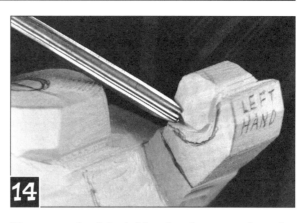

The inner side of the left hand and orange is formed by using a deep 4mm gouge or v-tool to make a deep groove between the orange and hand. This photo shows the groove already made.

To block out the right hand, first draw on the side view. Take a 4mm deep gouge and remove wood from the side of the orange. This will leave the outline of the thumb and finger.

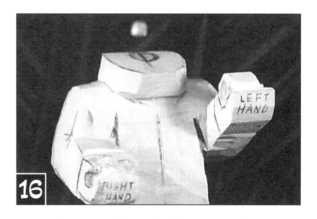

Use a calipers to make sure both hands are the same width. Are both oranges the same height and thickness? Do the right foot and leg match the left? Does the width of the collar match the pattern? Check the back as well. Are both shoulders the same thickness at the collar?

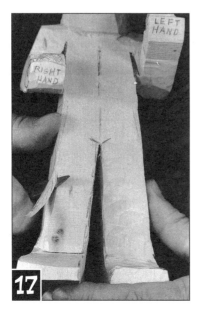

Once your blocked figure looks satisfactory, begin rounding the front corner of the right leg.

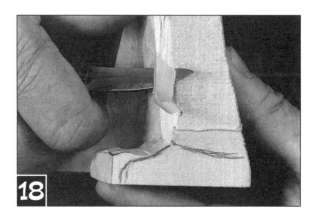

This photo shows the rounding of the front corner of the left leg. This photo was taken with a figure in an upright position, but for best results you should hold your carving upside down.

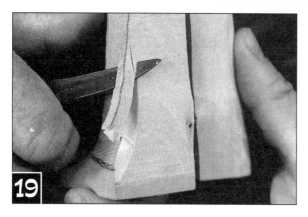

Round the back corner of the left leg and the inside corners along the back and front of the legs. Rotate your carving frequently.

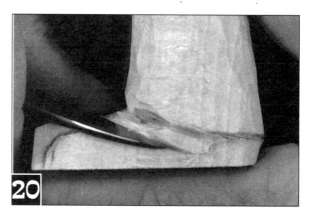

After rounding both legs, draw a line around the bottom of the pant legs and carve a notch to separate the foot from the pants. Repeat this process on the right leg. After you have completed the notch around both legs, use a carving knife to narrow the heels.

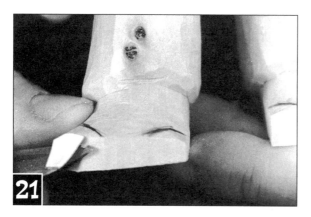

Use a pencil to draw on the shape of the toe, then use a carving knife to complete the shaping of the feet. My clown represents an early White Face Clown. The proper shoe for this figure is a tight fitting soft leather shoe.

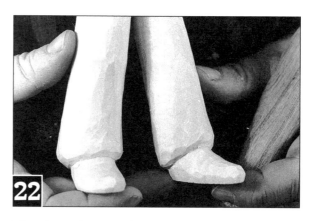

This photo shows nicely shaped feet ready for the final shoe detail.

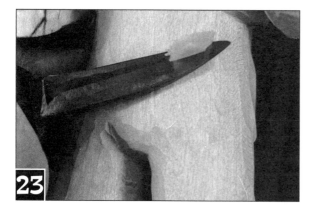

Using a woodcarving knife, do some rounding and shaping of the chest.

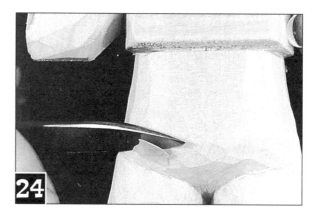

Next, round the buttocks and also the back. A carving knife works well for this step.

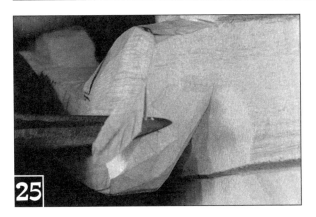

Use a carving knife to round the back of the arm. Repeat this process on both sides. In this photo, the right side has been completed, and I am now carving the left side.

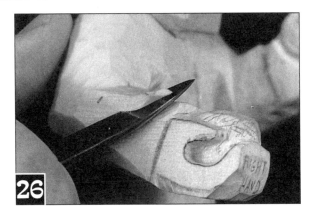

Next, use a carving knife to round the wrist and forearm. Repeat this process on both sides. Also round the front sides of the upper arms at this time.

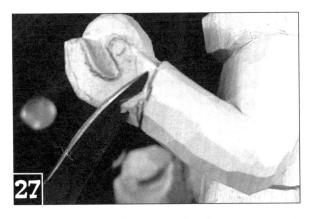

Draw a line around the wrist and make a stop cut on this line. Then remove a small amount of wood from the wrist making the wrist smaller than the shirt cuff. Repeat this process on the other arm.

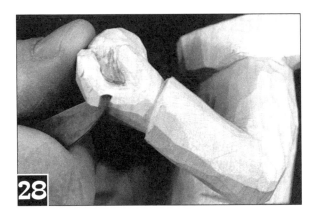

After both wrists are shaped, begin rounding the fingers on each hand and also the oranges.

To carve the head, first draw on the front view of the nose. Put a center line on the head if you did not do so earlier. Also draw a line around the bottom of the hat brim and outline the ears. Begin by removing wood from the right cheek between the nose and ear. Repeat this process on the left side.

When the cheeks appear to be nicely shaped, take your knife and remove wood along each side of the nose. The left side has been completed, and I am now carving the right side. Also angle the bottom of the nostrils upward on each side of the center line.

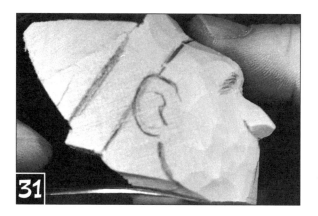

Using a carving knife, remove wood just below the ear where the neck and chin connect. You can also see how the nostrils were cut.

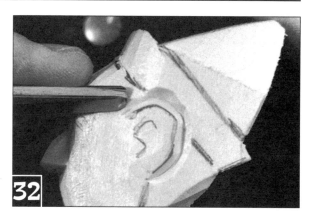

After shaping the upper neck a little closer to its desired shape, use an 8mm v-tool to outline the ear. Repeat this process on both sides.

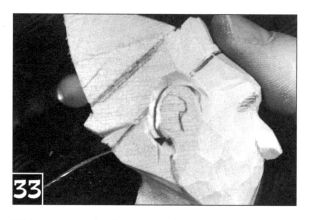

With a carving knife, remove the wood from behind each ear.

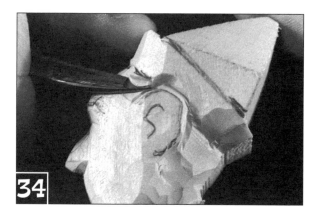

Also remove wood from above and in front of each ear. Narrow the hat brim behind the ears where it sits on the head.

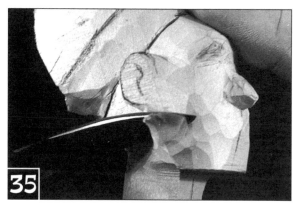

Next, remove wood in front of the ear and along the jaw and chin. Be careful not to point the chin too much. Repeat this process on the other side.

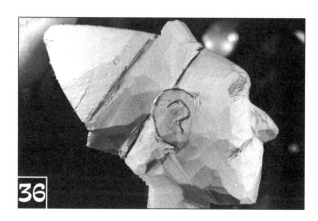

After these steps have been accomplished, you should have a matched pair of nicely blocked ears.

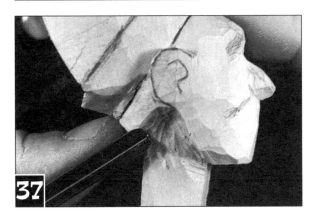

Next, use a 5mm medium gouge to remove a little more wood directly under the ear. This helps to shape the back of the jaw and the back of the skull.

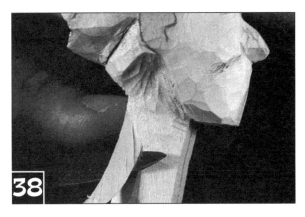

While working in this area, take a carving knife and round all four corners of the neck.

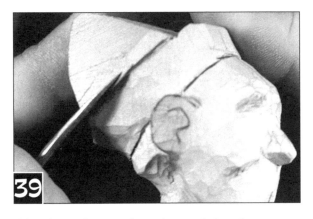

After the neck is satisfactorily rounded, make a stop cut along the top edge of the hat brim. This step should be done on both sides.

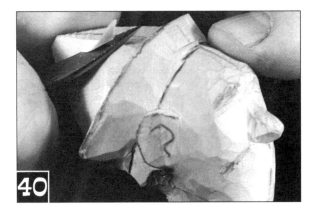

Block out the crown of the hat to match the front and side views of the pattern. Then use a carving knife to round all four corners of the hat crown.

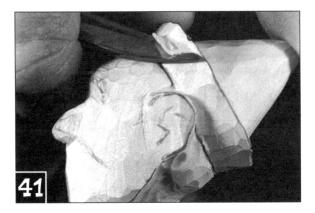

After nicely rounding the hat crown, you will also have four corners on the hat brim. These need to be rounded as well.

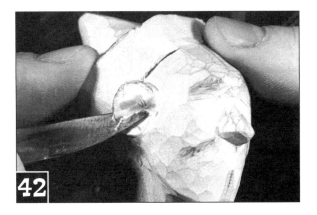

With the tip of your carving knife, angle the surface of the ear from the cheek to the outer edge of the ear. Repeat this step on the other side.

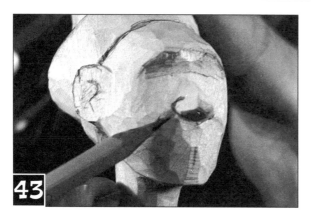

After shaping each side of the nose, use a pencil to draw on the curvature of the nostrils.

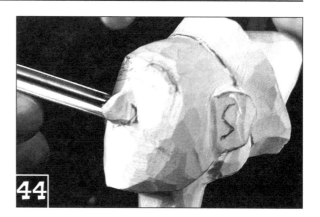

Using a 5mm medium gouge, make a stop cut around the nostrils. This cut is made by holding the head face-up and pushing straight down on the gouge.

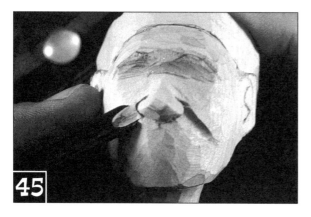

Using the same gouge, remove a small amount of wood from the cheeks on each side of the nostrils. The left side has been completed, and I am now working on the right side.

Begin shaping the area around the eyes. Draw lines for the eyebrows and along the area which will eventually be the lower eyelids.

I usually shape the eye sockets with a deep 4mm gouge. The upper and lower cuts on the left eye have been completed. I am now making the upper cut on the right eye.

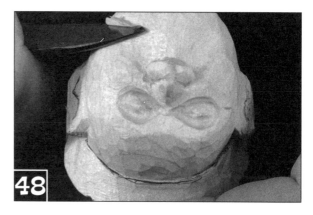

While holding the head upside down, shape and round the cheeks and chin. One side has been completed, and I am now working on the other side.

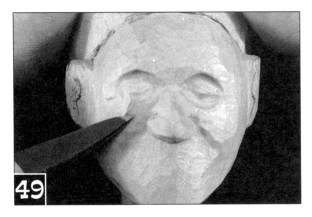

This photo shows the cheeks and chin nicely shaped and rounded. Now shape the top of the cheeks below the eyes.

Here, I am using my carving knife to smooth the forehead and eyebrows.

This practice block shows enlarged steps for carving the right eye.
A Draw an outline
B Smooth the eyeball with a knife tip
C Draw on the eyelids
D Outline the eye with a v-tool and knife
E Round the surface with a knife and draw the iris

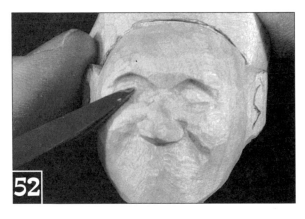

With the very tip of your knife, smooth the eyeball. The left eye has been smoothed, and I am now working on the right side. These are very tiny cuts. You should now have a smooth, protruding mound of wood in the center of the eye.

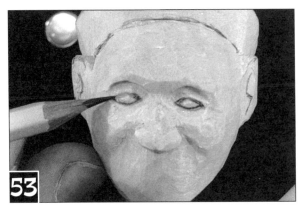

With a very sharp pencil, draw on the eyelids. Try to get them as even as possible.

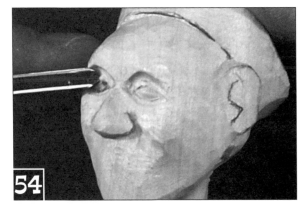

Use a small v-tool to outline the eye openings. Be sure to stay directly on the lines so both eyes will be the same size.

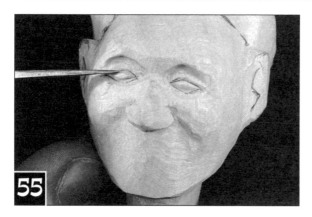

To make the eye openings as crisp as possible, let's take a very small, sharp knife and cut them a little deeper. You may have to hold the head in a different position than shown to be able to see what you are doing.

Using the same small knife, round the surfaces of the eyeballs. Deep, crispy cuts are important in the corners; the center of the eyeball should be round and protruding. Never make the center of the eye flat or deeper than the corners.

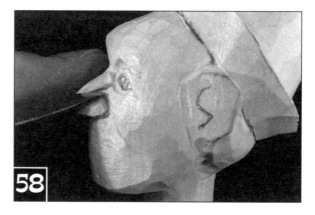

Just for fun, take a pencil and draw in the iris. Also in this photo, you can see that I have taken my knife and cleaned off the remaining centerline from the tip of the nose.

With the tip of your carving knife, remove a little wood along each side of the nose above the nostril to give the nose a better shape. Some instructors use a 5mm gouge for this step.

In this photo I have drawn on the mouth. I am now removing wood from just below the cheeks and along the chin to create a slight smile.

This block of scrap wood shows close-ups of how to carve lips.
A Draw on the lips.
B Separate the lips with a v-tool.
C Remove wood from the upper lips on each side of the filtrum.
D Remove wood from the lower lip curving it downward just below the filtrum.
E Use a gouge to indent the filtrum and remove wood below the bottom lip.

With a small v-tool, outline the mouth as shown in Step B of the practice block. Then follow steps C and D of the practice block.

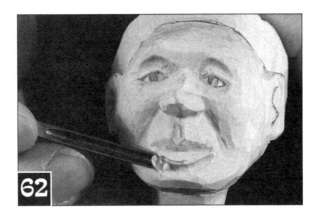

Next, use a small gouge to remove wood directly below the bottom lip. This cut will make a separation between the lower lip and chin, as in Step E on the practice block. A carving knife is used to smooth up the gouge marks and make everything flow together.

Use a 4mm gouge to carve the filtrum. For greater ease in carving, hold the figure upside down.

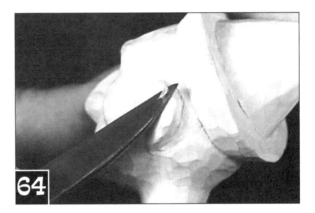

Finish rounding and shaping the ears.

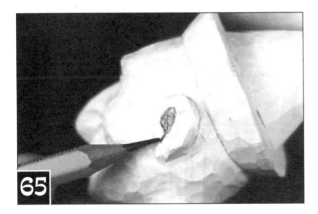

After final shaping of the ears, redraw on the ear opening.

Use a 4mm gouge to remove wood and form the inner ear.

Use a small v-tool to outline the skullcap. Then use a knife to trim the face area next to the skullcap.

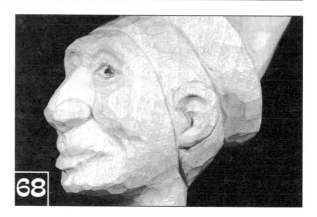

The clown head has been completed and is now ready for painting. The eyebrows will be covered with white facial make-up, then repainted to fit the clown's character, therefore, you do not need to carve them.

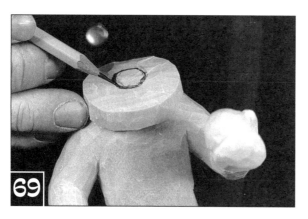

To attach the clown's head to the body, begin by drawing a circle the size of the neck in the center of the clown's collar.

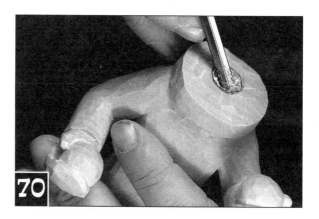

After making a good stop cut around this neckline, use your gouge and begin scooping a hole for the neck. Make clean, precise cuts. Do not twist or pry, or you may break your tool. Keep the stop cuts well ahead of the wood removal. A 1/4-inch depth will do nicely.

This photo shows a nice-fitting neck. Once you have a good fit, then you can begin to shorten the neck. Remove a small amount of wood at a time until the neck appears to be the proper length.

This photo shows a good fit, but do not glue the head to the body yet.

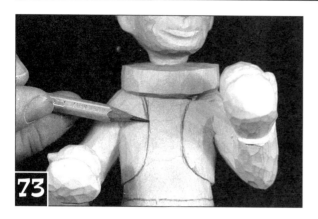

Use a pencil to draw the front of the jacket and the band around the top of the pants.

With a small v-tool outline the vest and also the top of the pants. You may want to hold your carving upside down to better accomplish this step.

In this photo, I am using a knife to remove wood from the chest and around the top of the pants. A very shallow gouge will also work nicely in the chest area; a knife tip will do a great job around the top of the pants.

To detail the collar, begin by drawing on the ruffles.

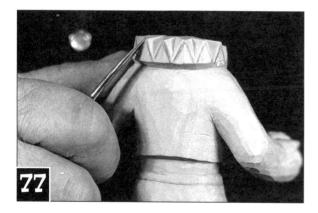

Use your carving knife to make notches around the top edge of the collar in between the ruffles.

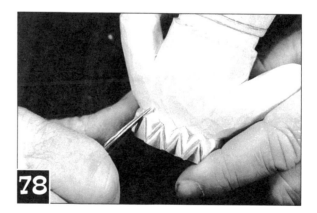

Next, hold the carving upside down and repeat the same process around the bottom or underside of the collar. Be careful not to make puncture marks in the clown's body.

This photo shows a nicely detailed collar. If you are satisfied with your ruffle, sharpen your knife and remove your penciled guidelines. Be careful not to remove too much wood.

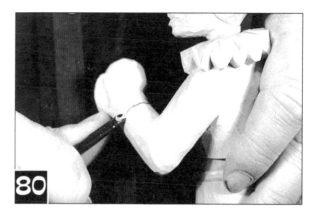

Draw a cuff line about 1/8-inch back from the end of his sleeve. Do this on both sleeves. Then use a small v-tool and make a groove around this cuff line. Stay directly on the line.

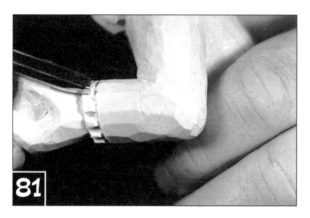

Use a very deep 4mm gouge to create a ruffle effect around the clown's cuffs.

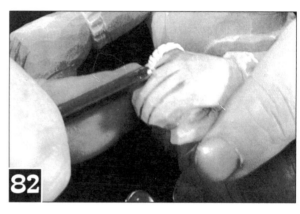

To finish the hands, use a pencil to draw on the fingers. With a small v-tool, carve directly on these lines to separate the fingers. You do not need to carve fingernails or knuckles on this figure, because White Face Clowns always wear gloves.

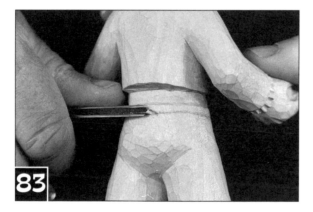

Use a small v-tool to complete the waistband around the top of the pants, front and back. Shape and smooth the waistband with the tip of your knife.

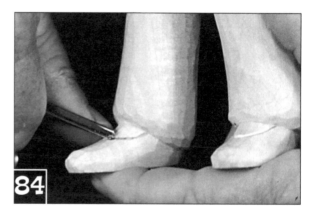

In this photo, I have drawn on the top of the shoes and used a small v-tool to outline the top of the shoe. The left foot has been completed, and I am now carving the right foot.

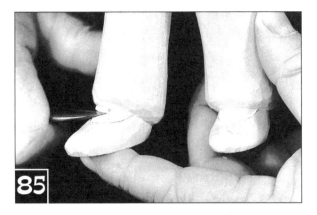

Use the tip of your knife to remove a very small amount of wood on the top of the foot.

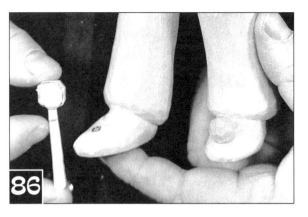

To make the fluffy tassels for the clown's shoes, take a small stick and carve a small ball on its end. Drill a 2mm hole in the top of the shoe. Then shorten and insert the stick into the hole.

Using a large v-tool, make wrinkles in the front bend of the arms. Also make small wrinkles where the arms attach to the shoulders.

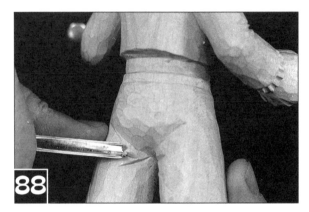

Still using a large v-tool, carve wrinkles under the buttocks and behind the knees.

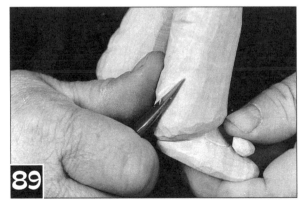

Use a knife or a large medium gouge to shape larger folds on the back of the legs. Use the tip of your knife to smooth up any wrinkles that appear too crisp. The finished edges of the wrinkles should be smooth. Also carve a few very shallow wrinkles in front, just below the knee along the outside of the leg.

Carve the third orange from a piece of scrap wood.

White Face Clown

Punch a hole in the orange held in the right hand, then insert a tiny piece of wire into the hole. Next punch a tiny hole into the third orange and mount it on the piece of wire. This will make the third orange appear to be suspended in mid-air.

This photo shows the back view of my nineteenth century White Face Clown. It is now carved and ready for painting. Refer to the painting instructions in the color section of this book and the notes at the beginning of this chapter for additional painting tips.

 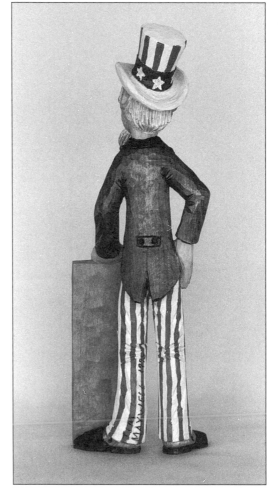

AMERICA'S FIRST FAMOUS CLOWN WAS THE immortal Dan Rice (1823–1900). He was a comic and strong man and also used small animals in his acts. He achieved lasting fame by wearing a brilliant costume in post Civil War political parades. His memorable suit of stars and stripes, large silk top hat and goatee beard became the prototype for the political cartoon we now call Uncle Sam. Yankee Dan is a big favorite of mine and his history makes him a must in any collection of clown figures.

CARVING TIPS

Blocking out Yankee Dan can be tricky. His body and sign are carved from one piece of wood; his head is carved from a second piece of wood. Step-

by-step instructions for blocking out the figure follow. You can use the steps outlined in the section on carving a White Face Clown to round and detail the blocked-out figure.

PAINTING NOTES

Most political cartoonists portray the modern day Uncle Sam as having a blue jacket, red and white striped pants, a red bow-tie and a red, white and blue top hat. Because this carving represents the modern day political character, he will not be wearing the white face make-up that Dan Rice (Yankee Dan) originally wore.

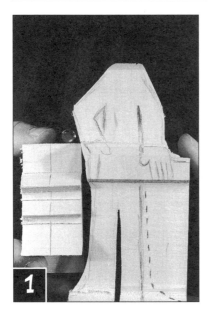

It is important to start this project with a blank that has accurate dimensions. Notice how I have drawn a dotted line to represent the left leg. The left foot turns out and is hidden behind the sign. Remember the grain of the wood must run vertically with the figure.

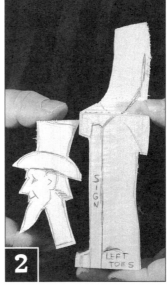

This photo shows the left side view. You can now see the edge of the sign and the portions of wood to be used for the left toes.

This photo shows the back view. I have marked the area of wood behind the sign which must be removed. You can now see clearly how the left foot turns outward behind the sign.

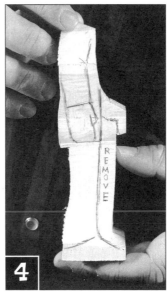

This photo shows the right side view. Notice that there is a great deal of wood to be removed in front of the right leg, across the stomach and over to the edge of the sign.

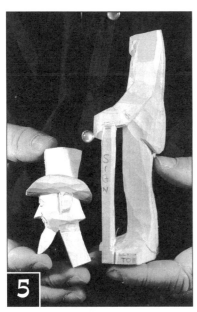

This photo shows the actual blocking completed. As you can see, this left side view shows I have removed enough wood to separate the sign from the left leg. The sign is connected to the figure at the left toes and left hand only.

This right side view shows the right leg and chest area at its correct dimension, ready for final rounding and detailing. Check all your dimensions carefully, then round the carving.

This photo shows a nicely rounded Yankee Dan. The head has been properly fitted to the body, and the figure is now ready for final detailing.

This photo shows the detailing completed. Yankee Dan is now ready for painting.

Auguste Clown

AFTER THE TURN OF THE TWENTIETH CENTURY, THE circus had grown in popularity. A successful show would have employed several clowns. In order to create new and original personalities, clowns began using a variety of colors on their faces and allowing some flesh to show. They also used large rubber noses and cut holes in their skull-caps to allow ridiculously colored hair to protrude through the holes. Their costumes became large, baggy garbs of mix-matched colors, stripes and polka dots. Oversized shoes and other props became part of the act for this new type of clown, called the Auguste, which means funny or goofy.

My Auguste pattern bears some facial similarities to Lou Jacobs, a famous Ringling Brothers clown. The costume colors resemble those of my friend "Chicken Lips," a well known clown of the Kansas City area.

CARVING TIPS
The following pages outline the steps for blocking out the body and head of an Auguste Clown. Round and detail your figure based on the steps used to create a White Face Clown.

PAINTING NOTES
The Auguste Clown uses a wide variety of material patterns, but many are difficult to paint on a figure of this size. Checks, squares and polka dots can be used if kept at a reasonable size. Some simple flower patterns can be used. Complicated or multi-colored material patterns should be avoided.

Old circus posters and books on clowning provide an endless variety of Auguste clown faces, if you wish to create your own clown personalities. If not, then you can follow the traditional design of my Auguste clown face.

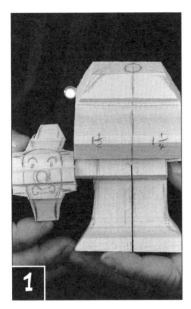

To block out the Auguste Clown, begin by sawing the side view of the blank. Notice that the front view center line is offset to the left. This allows extra wood for the right hand and makes it possible to position the large drum between the right hand and left foot.

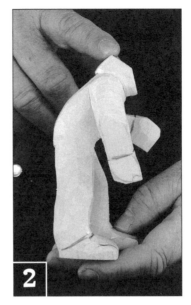

This photo shows the right side view.

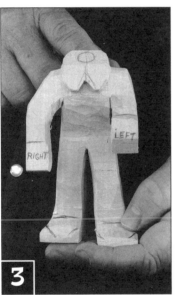

This photo shows the front view. Notice that the right arm is extended outward and to the right to accommodate the thickness of the drum.

This photo shows the front view with the drum.

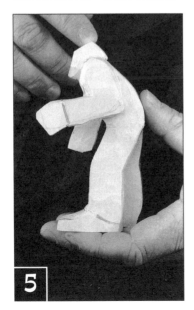

Once the Auguste Clown has been blocked out, begin shaping the body by following the same steps used on the White Face Clown. Check the dimensions twice. It is very important to be as accurate as possible when you start.

When blocking the head, follow the instructions for the White Face Clown. This photo shows a front view of the blocked-out head. Leave a great deal of wood to be shaped into hair behind the ears. The hair and ears should be blocked in one step.

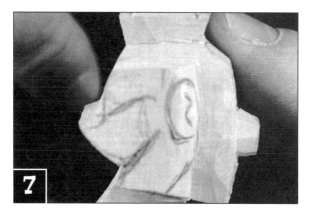

This photo shows a side view of the hair and ear.

Use a large v-tool to outline the ears.

Use a carving knife to remove wood from the side of the hair to make the ear stand out just a little.

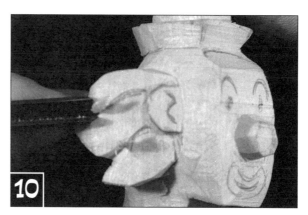

After removing enough wood to make the ears stand out from the hair, redraw the locks of hair. Separate these locks with a large v-tool.

This photo shows a nicely blocked head that is now ready for rounding, shaping and detailing. Follow the steps for carving the White Face Clown if you need additional instructions.

Black Face Clown

THE BLACK FACE CLOWN IS A UNIQUE VERSION OF the Auguste Clown. He is sometimes referred to as a character clown. He is the third type of clown and was made very popular in America by such famous performers as Red Skelton and Emmett Kelly.

This butterfly catcher is my attempt at creating a new Black Face character. He bears the traditional image of one who tries very hard at what he does, but accomplishes very little. Black Face Clowns are quick to win love and sympathy with any crowd, as well as the heart of this woodcarver. They are one of my all-time favorite subjects.

CARVING TIPS
Step-by-step instructions for blocking out, rounding and detailing this figure are shown on the following pages. The head, body, butterflies and net are all carved from separate pieces of wood.

PAINTING NOTES
Since this Black Face character clown is busy trying to catch butterflies, a flowered design shirt will enhance the theme. His pants and shoes are earth tones, and he has red suspenders and colorful print patches. Refer to the color photos when painting the sad face. The butterflies are an important part of the overall theme, so we used photographs of real butterflies as a color guide.

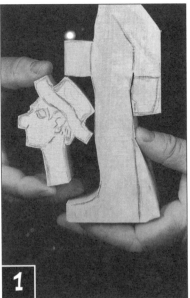

To carve the Black Face Clown, I used a piece of basswood that was 4x4x11. Trace the pattern of the clown on the wood. Bandsaw the side views first. Remember the grain should run vertically.

1

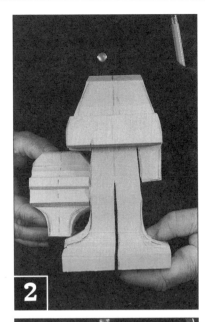

The front views and center line have been drawn on the blank and the excess wood along the sides has been removed with a band saw. A little extra wood has been allowed on the right arm.

2

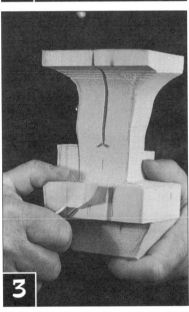

Next draw on the width of the right hand and remove the excess wood along the chest. I am holding the carving upside down and using my knife. You may also clamp the figure in a vise and use a shallow gouge to perform the blocking steps.

3

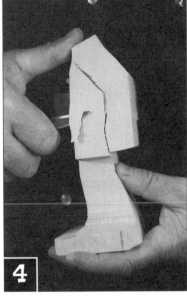

Draw on the side view of the left arm and begin removing excess wood in front of the left arm. This step can be done with a knife or a shallow gouge.

4

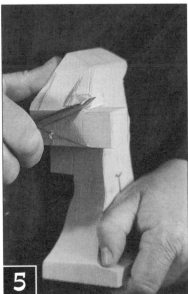

Draw on the side view of the right arm. Use a knife and a shallow gouge to block out the area in front of the upper arm.

5

I am holding the carving upside down to remove the wood under the right arm.

6

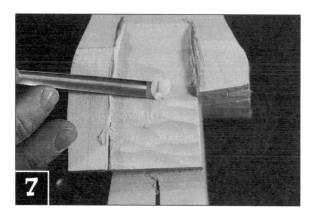

Draw on the back view of the arms. Make stop cuts along the arms and use a shallow gouge to remove the wood. You should have a saw cut running over the top of the buttocks and part way up the back from when you sawed out the blank. Carve deep enough to reach this cut.

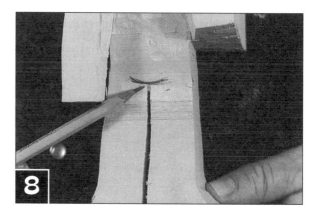

This photo shows how much wood must come off of the back. I have drawn a line for the buttocks and sawed a little higher between the legs.

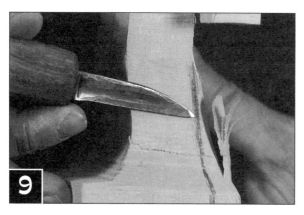

Draw on the back view of the left leg. Then, remove wood from the back of the left leg, using a knife or shallow gouge.

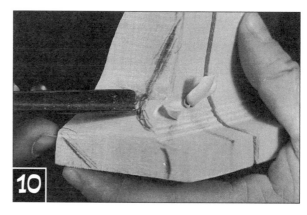

Now, draw on the side view of the right leg. It bends at the knee, and the heel is raised above the floor, so remove wood from in front of the right leg and right foot. A deep gouge works best for this step.

Use a pencil to draw on the top view of the feet. Many Black Face Clowns wear professionally made large clown shoes.

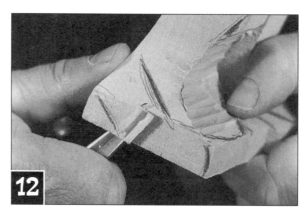

Use a knife to block the right heel. Also repeat this step on the left heel.

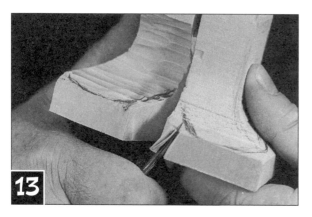

Block the inside corners of both feet.

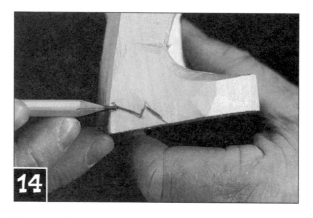

Draw on the right heel. It is raised slightly from the floor.

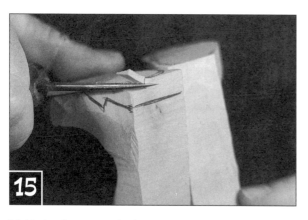

Hold the figure upside down and remove the excess wood from beneath the heel of the right foot.

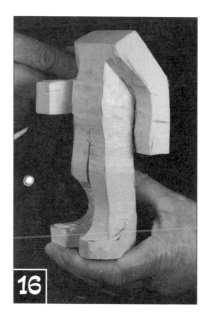

This photo shows a nicely blocked figure.

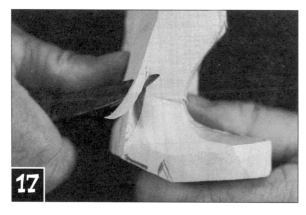

Begin rounding the figure using a carving knife. I have started on the back corner of the right leg.

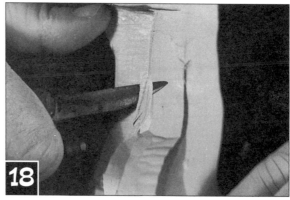

Still using a knife, round the front corners of the right leg.

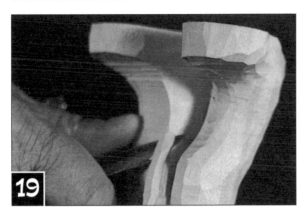

Hold the figure upside down to round the inside front corner of the left leg.

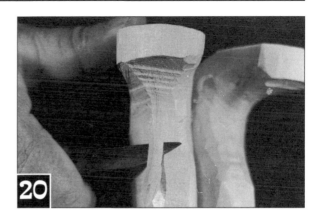

Hold the figure upside down to round the outside front corner of the left leg. Round the back outside corner of the left leg in the same manner. Rotate the carving so that the cuts always work well with the grain. Check closely for any corners you may have missed.

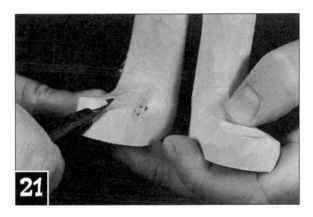

Before rounding and shaping the toe on the right foot, use calipers to check the length of the foot. Remember that the right foot is positioned somewhat behind the left. Repeat the rounding process on the left foot. Try to get both feet the same size.

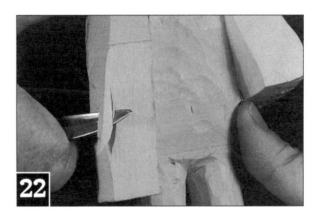

Begin rounding the back corners of the left arm.

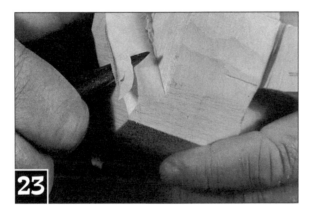

Hold your carving upside down to easily round the front corners of the left arm.

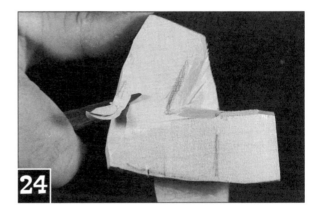

Round the back corners of the right arm.

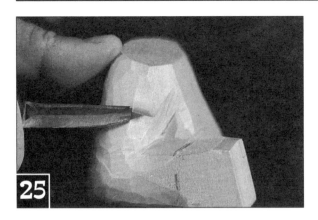

Round the front corners of the right arm.

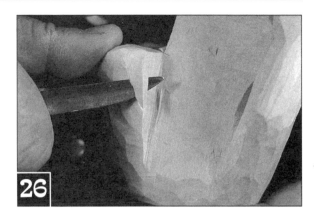

Rotate the carving to an upside down position and remove wood from the back corner of the right arm.

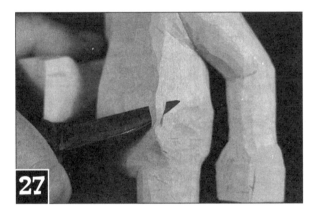

Begin rounding the upper torso on the front corners.

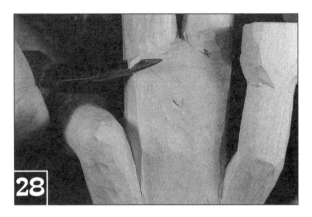

Hold the figure upside down to round and shape the buttocks and back. You will need to turn and rotate the figure many times to have the best carving advantage for shaping the body.

This photo shows a nicely shaped body now ready for detailing. The head should be fitted before the final detailing can be completed, so begin working on the head now.

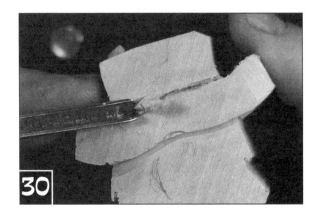

To carve the head, first draw on the brim of the hat. Do this on both sides. Use your v-tool to make a stop cut along the upper and lower edge of the brim.

Check your pattern carefully, then draw on the width of the crown. Use your knife to remove wood from each side of the crown, making frequent stop cuts.

Use a calipers to check the width of the ears. Draw these measurements on the front of the head.

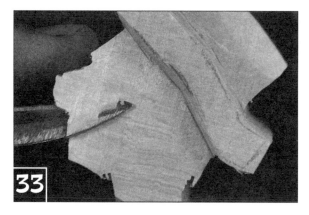

Now use a knife to remove wood from each side of the head until the head is the desired thickness. Make stop cuts well in advance of your knife cuts along the bottom of the hat brim.

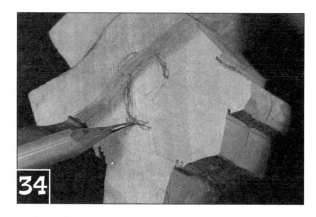

Redraw the ears.

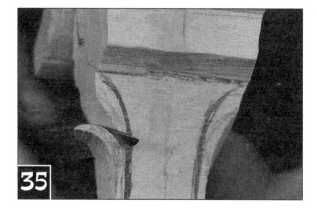

Draw on the front view of the neck and block the neck with your carving knife. This step may be easier if you hold the head upside down.

In this photo, I have drawn on the round rubber nose, and I am using the carving knife to remove wood from the corners of the face, between the nose and ears.

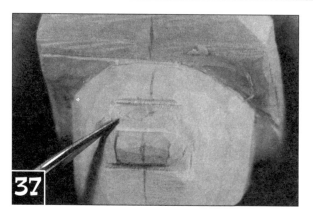

Use a carving knife to shape the rubber nose. The left side has been completed, and I am now shaping the right side.

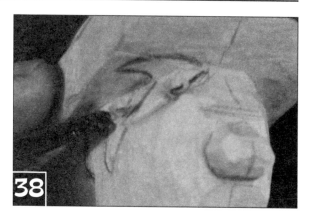

Next, draw on the hair, then outline it with your v-tool. Study the pattern closely. The hair will partly cover each ear. Also outline the lower part of the ear as well at this time.

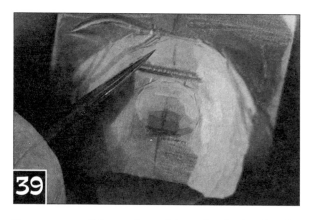

Remove a small layer of wood from the forehead and upper cheeks to make the hair stand out.

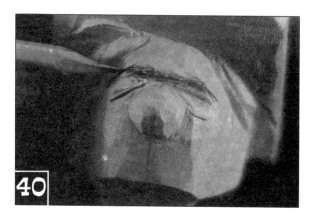

Use a pencil to draw the eyebrow across the forehead.

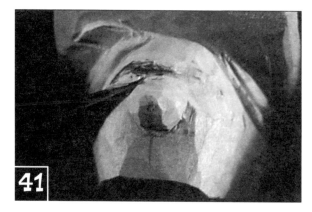

Take your knife and make a small concave area for each eye. The left side has been completed, and I am now working on the right side.

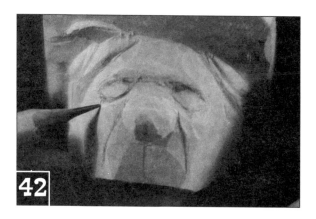

Redraw the actual shape of the eyes onto the concave areas that were just completed in the preceding step. Do not arch the upper contours of the eyes too much. Keep in mind that this is a sad face clown.

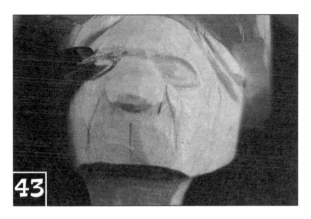

Use a 4mm gouge to shape the eye mounds. To complete the eye detail, just follow the step-by-step procedures of the enlarged carving aid on eyes.

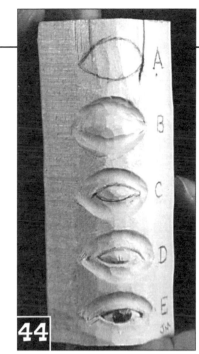

This practice block shows enlarged steps for carving the right eye.
A Draw an outline
B Smooth the eyeball with a knife tip
C Draw on the eyelids
D Outline the eye with a v-tool and knife
E Round the surface with a knife and draw the iris

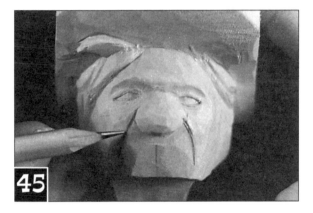

After completing the eyes, draw on the facial lines for the mouth. Begin at the nostril and go down across the cheek.

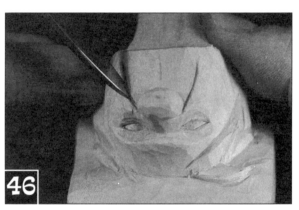

Hold the head upside down and make a stop cut on the facial lines using the tip of your knife.

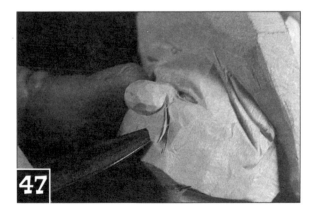

Use the tip of your knife to remove wood just inside the facial lines.

Draw on the mouth. A sad face mouth should curve slightly downward at the edges.

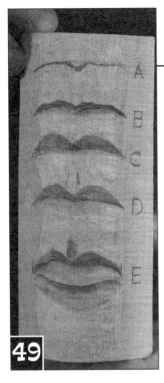

49

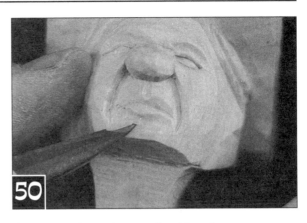

50

This photo shows enlarged steps for cutting sad face lips.
A Draw on the lips.
B Separate the lips with a v-tool.
C Remove wood from the upper lips on each side of the filtrum.
D Remove wood from the lower lip, curving it downward just below the filtrum.
E Use a gouge to indent the filtrum. Also use a gouge to remove wood below the bottom lip.

This photo shows the completed lips. I am now using a carving knife to smooth the chin.

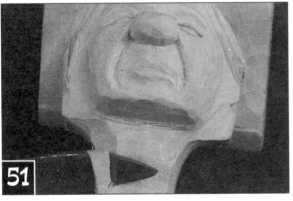

51

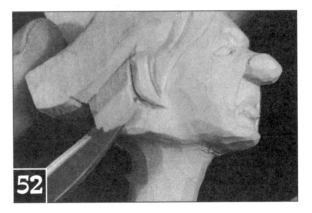

52

Now, round all four corners of the neck.

Once satisfied with the shape of the face, begin carving the area behind the ears. Make a stop cut around the back of the ears and remove some wood from each side of the head behind and below the ears.

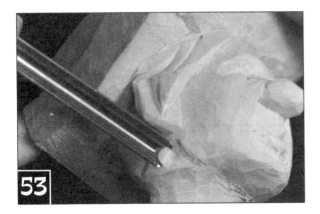

53

54

Use a 5mm gouge to remove wood from directly below the ears along the neck. This will help to shape the jaw and hairline.

At this stage, finish the hat before actually detailing the hair. Begin by rounding all four corners of the hat brim.

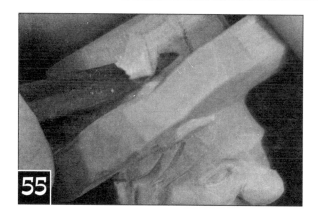

Next, round all four corners of the hat crown.

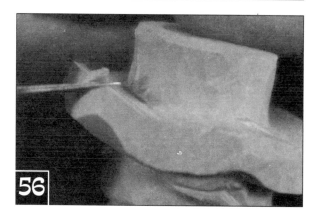

Thin the hat brim to its desired thickness with a carving knife. A 5mm gouge works well on top of the hat brim to scoop in a few wrinkles and create a crumpled look.

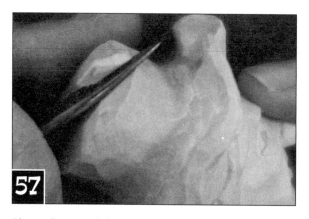

Shape the top of the crown.

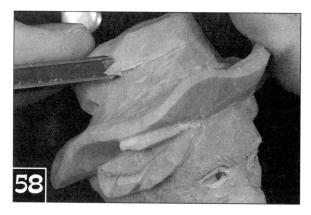

Use a large v-tool to make big wrinkles in the crown of the hat.

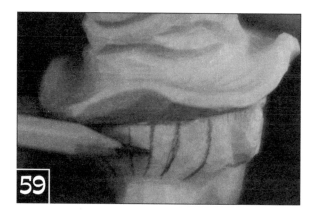

Now, detail the hair. Begin by drawing large sections or locks, which angle downward toward the center of the neck.

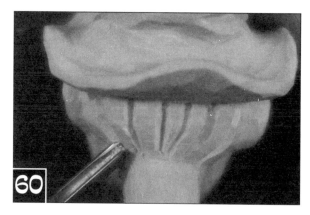

Use a v-tool to separate the locks of the hair. Use random sizes. Rotate the head frequently for ease in carving.

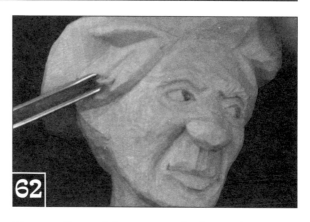

Use a small v-tool for texturing these locks of hair. After texturing, use a small sharp knife to separate the points of each lock. It is not necessary to point every follicle.

Use a small v-tool for texturing the hair in front.

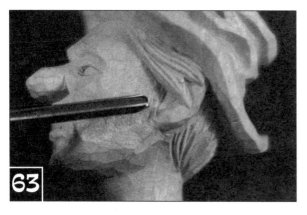

Use a 2mm deep gouge to shape the inside of the left ear. The right ear is covered with hair. If your clown has a right ear showing, than you will need to shape it also.

Carve the eyebrows with a 1mm deep gouge or small v-tool. Eyebrows are important on a sad face caricature. They do not have the high arches of the White Face or Auguste Clown. I like thin faces for sad face clowns, so I have trimmed the cheeks just a little more.

To attach the head, draw a circle the same size as the neck on the clown's shoulders. Make a hole and attach the head following the same steps and procedures used on the White Face Clown. Don't be over confident.

After fitting the head, use a knife to smooth and round the shoulders. The head does not need to be in place while rounding and shaping the shoulders.

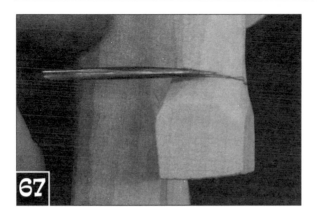

To shape the hands, begin by drawing a line around the shirt sleeve cuffs. Then use a carving knife to make a shallow stop cut on this line. Do this on both hands.

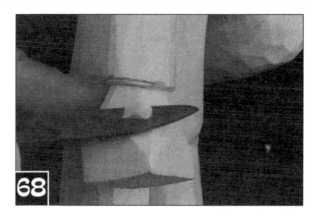

Use a carving knife to remove wood from each wrist, cutting toward the stop cut.

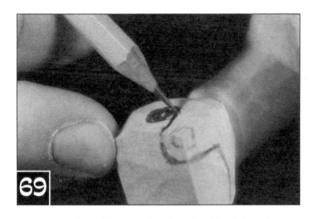

Use a pencil to draw on the thumb of both hands.

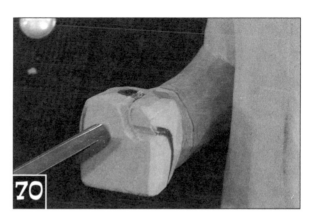

Outline the thumb with a v-tool.

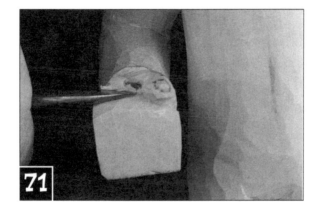

Use a knife to remove wood from the top of the hand, but not the thumb. This will make the thumb appear to be higher than the fingers.

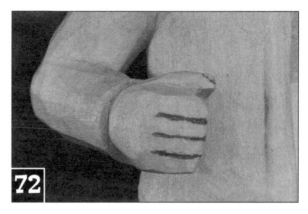

A little more work with the carving knife, and the right hand is now ready for finger detail.

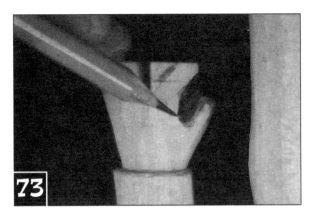

To carve the left hand, first draw on the front view and remove wood between the thumb and fingers with a 2mm deep gouge. I have penciled in the area where I am removing the wood. This photo shows the process partially completed.

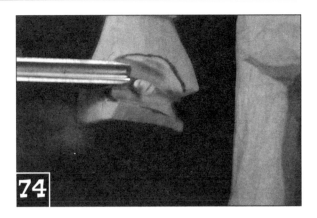

Use a small deep gouge to remove wood from the palm of the left hand. Be careful not to break the thumb.

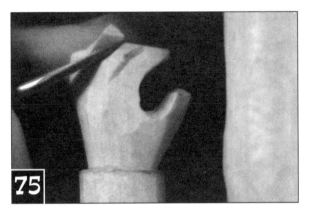

Hold the carving upside down to shape the knuckles on the left hand. You can now see that the entire area of wood between the thumb and fingers has been removed.

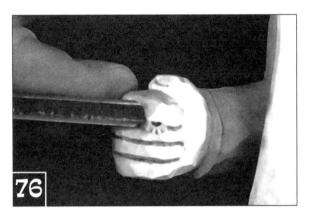

After both hands have been nicely shaped, draw on the fingers and use your v-tool for detailing.

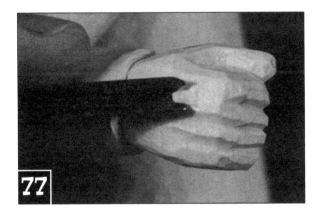

Add a little shape to the back of the knuckles with a 5mm gouge. These are shallow cuts.

Most Black Face Clowns do not wear gloves, so you may want to put fingernails and knuckles on the hands.

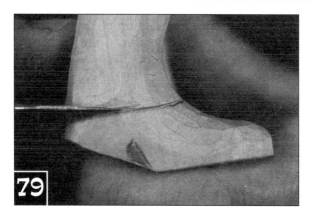

To detail the feet, draw a line around the pant cuff. With a knife, make a stop cut on this line.

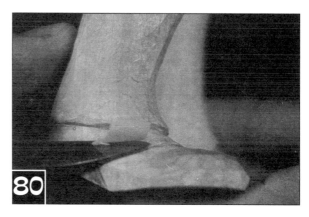

Use a knife to remove wood just below the pant cuff, cutting upward toward the stop cut.

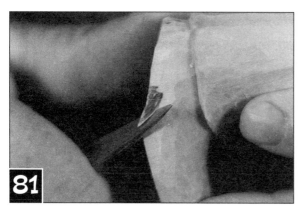

Make a notch for the heel with a knife.

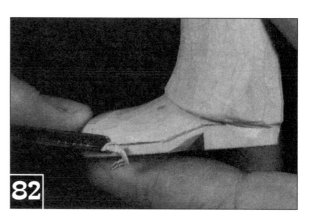

Draw a line for the sole of the shoe and outline it with a small v-tool.

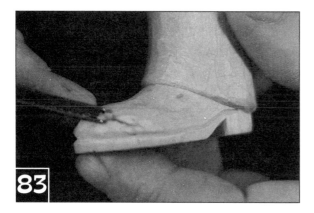

To make it appear that the clown has a hole in his shoe, draw a line across the left toe and use a small v-tool to make a cut along the line.

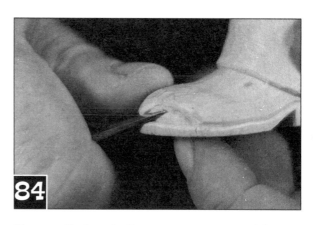

Use a small, sharp knife to remove some wood from the toe. Make it appear recessed in the opening.

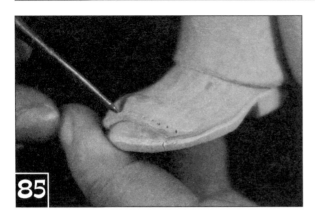

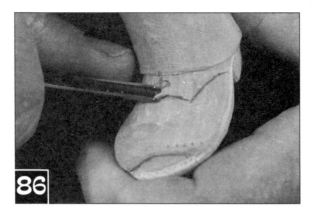

Use an awl to punch stitching holes around the opening to make it appear that the end of the shoe has come unsewn.

Draw detailing on the instep of the shoe and carve it with your v-tool.

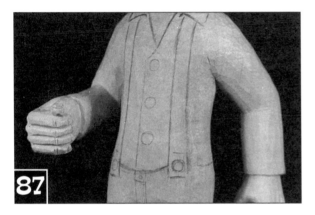

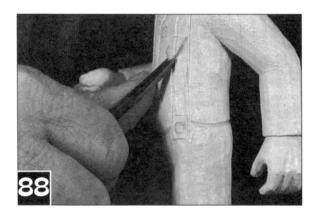

To detail the clothing on the Black Face Clown, start by drawing the neck opening and collar of the shirt. Draw on some suspenders and the top of the pants. Add buttons for the shirt or a comical necktie.

Use a v-tool to outline the clothing.

To make the suspenders stand out just a little, use a carving knife to remove wood along each side of the suspenders.

Trim around the collar on the shoulders to make the collar appear thicker.

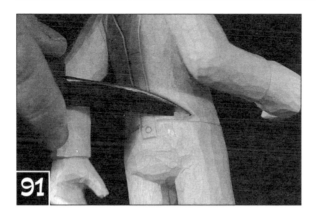

Use a carving knife to remove wood from the shirt around the top of the pants.

A 4mm gouge works well for making a clown's exaggerated buttons. To make a button, push the gouge straight into the chest (button A). Then remove wood around the button with the gouge (button B). Be very careful not to pop out the center of the button.

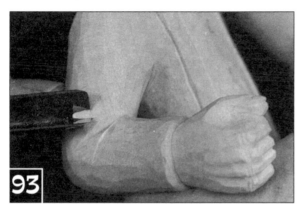

Use a large v-tool to make wrinkles in the front bends of the arms.

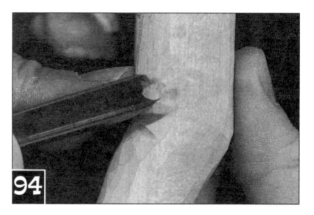

Use a large v-tool to make wrinkles behind the bends of the knees.

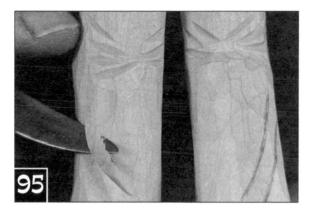

In this photo, I am carving large wrinkles on the back of the legs. They run diagonal from the back of the ankle to the side of the knee. Also shown in this photo are small wrinkles beneath the buttocks and on the pants where the suspenders are buttoned.

Use a knife to make a few diagonal wrinkles leading from the elbows upward and downward on the arms.

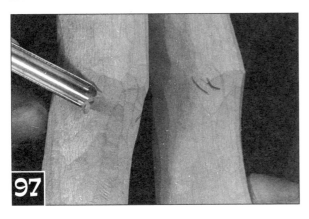

Use a 5mm gouge to make some small wrinkles in front, below the knees. This photo also shows some small wrinkles on the bottom of the pant leg that were made with a large v-tool.

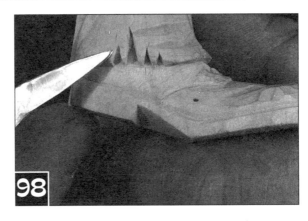

Use a small sharp knife to make a few ragged tears in the bottom of the pant legs.

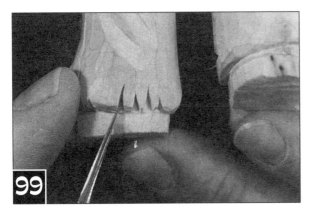

Make these cuts on the back of the pants as well.

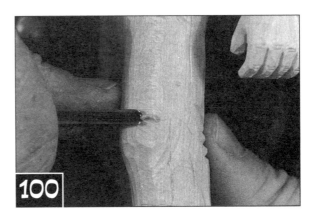

Use a small v-tool to make patches on the knees and elbows. You may wish to outline them with a pencil first.

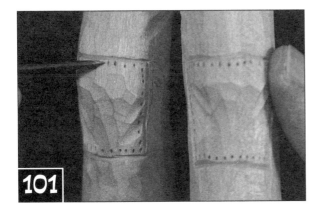

Use an awl to make stitching on the patches.

My Black Face Clown is using a butterfly net and butterflies for his props. Follow the pattern to block out the butterfly net. Use standard carving procedures for completing the net.

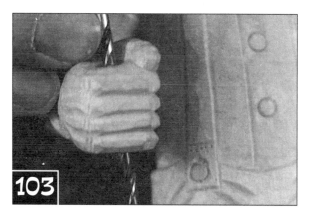

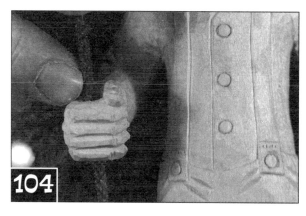

Using a small hand drill, make a hole through the right hand. Sometimes I use a 2mm gouge. Be extremely careful, when applying pressure; you don't want to break or split the hand.

Use a small riffler file for final fitting and to correct the alignment of the butterfly net.

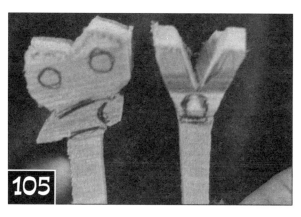

This photo shows two butterflies bandsawed from both a front and side view. Leave the butterflies on a small stick until they are completely carved. The stick will serve as a dowel for attaching the butterflies to the clown. Be careful here not to cut your fingers.

To mount your butterflies on the clown, drill a small hole. Then, trim the stick on the end of the butterfly to fit the hole. Do not glue the butterflies to the figure until after you have painted them. You may want to make several butterflies and place them in different positions.

This photo shows the finished clown, now ready for painting.

Rodeo Clown

RODEO CLOWNS USUALLY APPEAR AS BLACK FACE or Auguste Clowns, but these fellows are much more than just funny clowns. The most important part of their job is actually not performing as a clown, but drawing a charging bull's attention away from thrown or injured cowboys. To be a Rodeo Clown, one must first have great courage and also be in great physical condition. Since cowboy and western art has such great appeal, I have included my pattern of a Rodeo Clown in this collection.

CARVING TIPS
Follow the normal carving procedures when carving the Rodeo Clown. His head is carved separately and turned to one side. I used a few large choppy knife cuts to give the appearance of a bat-

tered hat. This little clown has a tough job, but concealing his body in a barrel makes him easy to carve.

PAINTING NOTES
Rodeo clowns always wear western clothing and most any design would work well on this figure. I have chosen a white shirt with blue stripes and a red scarf with white dots. He has a tan hat. Choosing either the Auguste or Black Face make-up would be appropriate for this figure.

Carving Clowns

Painting Clowns

Painting the clown face is probably the most important part of any clown project. Your clown will at first appear to be just another woodcarving until the face has been painted. It is the facial paint which gives the clown his personality.

In the following pictures, Margie will be showing the painting steps for the three basic clown faces, plus additional steps for painting an Auguste Clown costume. She will be showing some special tips for detailing patches, floral patterns and other small objects.

Margie has used the following paints and supplies for painting the projects in this book:

Paints (Tube Acrylic): Yellow Oxide, red oxide, hookers green, burnt umber, burnt sienna, iridescent silver, titanium white, mars black, cadmium red medium, cobalt blue, cadmium yellow medium, flesh, folk art, skintone.

Brushes (royal sable): sizes 0 round, 2 round, 2 flat, 4 flat, 6 flat, 8 flat

Herkie, an antique ventriloquist dummy, gets an August Clown face, painted by Margie at her work table. Herkie has a warm smile for all who visit at Maxwell's Woodcarving Shop in Cole Camp, Missouri.

To paint the White Face Clown, use a #4 or #6 flat brush to paint the entire face, including the ears, eyes, and skullcap. Use white paint that has been thinned slightly. After the white face has dried, apply the blue iris in his eyes, with your smallest size round brush.

Use a 4-H hard-leaded pencil to lightly draw on the make-up design. Paint all the red areas first. Thin the red paint slightly, but don't allow the white undercoat to show through.

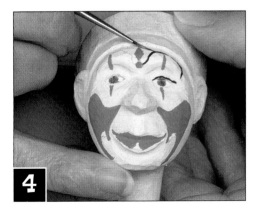

Now apply the second color, black, to the eyebrows and eyelids with a round #2 brush. While working in this area, add a small dot of white to the blue iris for a highlight. Early White Face Clowns used only red and black make-up on their all white faces.

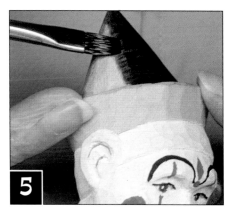

After completing the clown's face, begin painting the hat. The crown is painted a dark green, with a #6 flat brush.

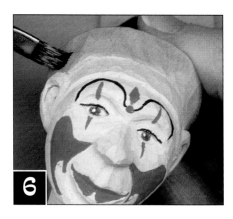

The brim is painted a yellow green with a #6 flat brush.

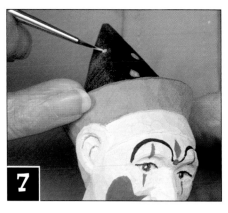

The smaller detail of the yellow and white dots are painted on last with a small round brush.

The White Face Clown head, painted with personality and character, is now finished. The remaining color schemes for painting the body are included with the carving instructions.

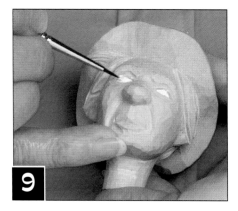

To paint the Black Face Clown, begin by painting the whites of his eyes with a small round brush.

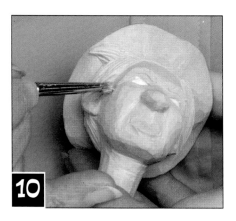

The flesh color, which has been thinned slightly, is being applied here with a #4 flat brush.

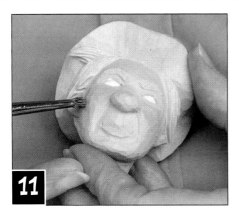

The cheeks are highlighted by combining a very small amount of red with the flesh color in a mixing container and then applying it very sparingly on the cheeks. Apply this color while the flesh undercoat is still wet.

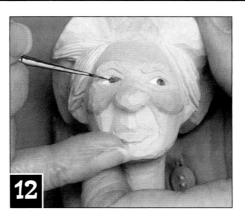

Apply the iris color with a small round brush. By putting the iris in the left hand corners, your clown will appear to be watching for elusive butterflies.

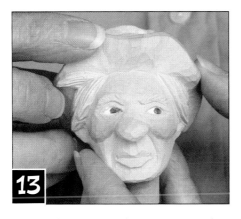

With flesh and eyes painted, we're now ready to apply the more distinctive details of his character face.

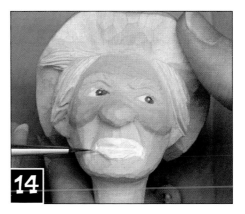

The white mouth, with its sad drooping corners, is the most important part of this Black Face Character. This white needs to be thick enough to cover the flesh undercoat. A small dot of white can also be applied to the iris at this time.

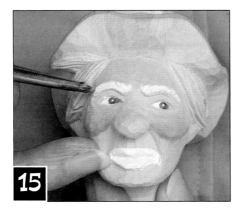

Eyebrows are applied with a #2 flat brush. Be careful not to arch them too much, since this is a sad face clown. Exaggerrated arches will make the clown look happy.

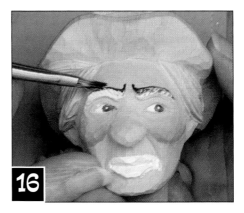

Black paint is applied along the tops of the eyebrows. This feature is also an important part of the clown's sad look.

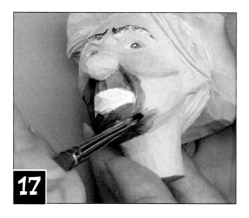

Apply the black face made-up with a #2 flat brush. Thin the black paint quite a bit.

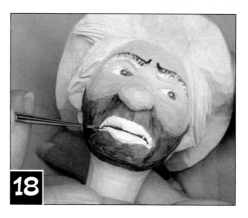

While your black paint is handy, take a small round brush and paint a separation line between the lips.

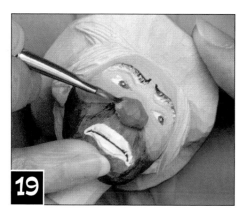

Let's take a #2 flat brush and paint the large red rubber nose.

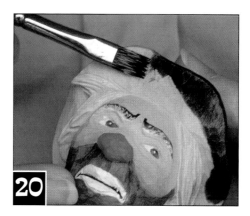

With the face completed, now paint the hat black with a #6 flat brush. Use a very thin paint.

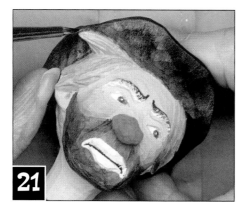

The hair is painted a golden yellow and is highlighted with a small amount of white, which has been applied with an almost dry brush.

This photo shows a completed Black Face Clown head.

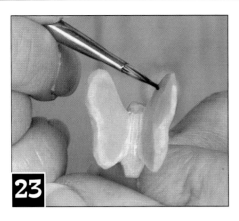

To paint the butterfly, begin by applying yellow to the wings.

Next paint the black areas with a small round brush.

Then, using a toothpick, apply tiny white dots directly on the black.

Painting the floral design may appear a bit difficult, but this unique design can be easily achieved using the following steps. First paint the entire shirt a light color, then choose a base color for the five pointed petal-like flowers, which are painted here with a #2 round brush.

Next use your smallest round brush to paint a black center in each petal.

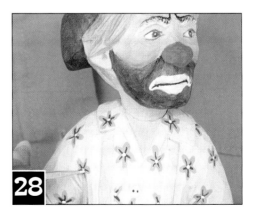

Then with a pointed toothpick, put a small white dot on the center of each flower.

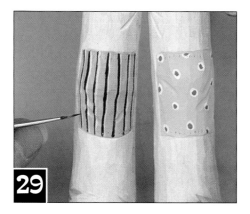

You may also want to add colorful patches to your clown by adding the base color first. The patches are then painted with colorful accents. You can have fun here creating an endless variety of material designs.

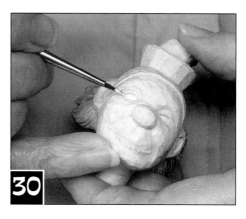

To paint the Auguste Clown face, begin by painting the whites of his eyes, with a small round brush.

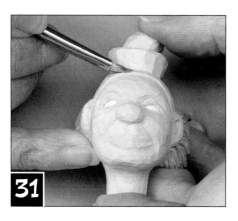

Next, paint the face and skull cap with your flesh color slightly thinned.

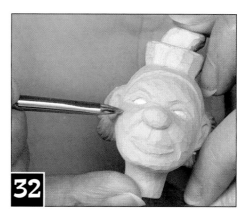

Highlight the cheeks by mixing a small amount of red and the flesh color in a separate container. Apply this color to the cheeks while the flesh undercoat is still wet.

In this photo, the color of the iris has just been applied with a small round brush.

Use slightly thinned white to paint the mouth area and the area above the eyes. Most real Auguste Clowns paint their white make-up to match the contours of their face. This is how their individual personality and character is developed.

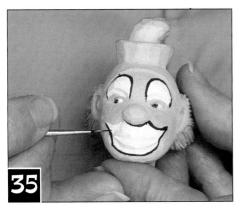

Use a small round brush to paint on the highly arched black eyebrows and make a black outline around the mouth area.

The smiling lips have now been painted on with a small round brush. Next, paint the red rubber nose. Then thin your red paint some more and paint his hat.

The hair color is red oxide, thinned, and applied with a #2 flat brush.

Add a sparkle to the clown's eyes by painting a tiny white dot on the iris. The Auguste Clown face is now completed.

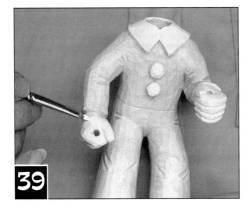

To paint the Auguste Clown body, use a #2 flat brush and paint his collar, gloves and fluffy tassels white.

Paint the clown's costume with light blue paint, thinned slightly, applied with a #6 flat brush.

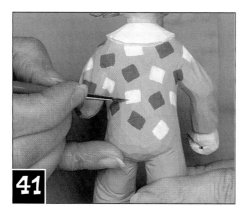

To create the colorful patch-work pattern used on this Auguste Clown, apply the red and the white squares by rotating the colors continuously to achieve an equal amount of each color.

Next outline the squares with a small narrow black line applied with your smallest round brush. Also apply the black accent lines at the collar.

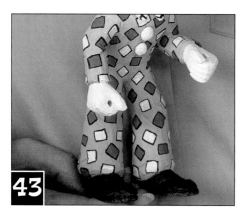

Paint the shoes black and the Auguste Clown is now ready for antiquing.

When the carving is dry, apply an antiquing finish. Squeeze approximately 1/2 inch of this burnt umber oil color from the paint tube and then mix it with the 1 cup of linseed oil. Shake or stir until it becomes totally mixed. The thin mixture is then applied over the entire clown, with an old brush.

Wipe the carving dry with a soft cloth. Be sure you remove all antiquing from the wrinkles and undercuts. You can also use an old dry brush to help clean hard to reach areas. *Rags containing linseed oil will spontaneously combust and are extremely dangerous, unless kept in an air tight container, at all times.*

Tramp Clown

FREDDIE FREELOADER WAS A BLACK FACE TRAMP Clown created by Red Skelton. I have loved Freddie's performances since I was a boy. From these fond old memories I have created this Tramp Clown pattern, which I call City Dump. There are many such lovable characters in the clown profession. Some of my other favorites are firemen and policemen.

CARVING TIPS

The Tramp Clown is a very old pattern designed years ago and is intended to be an easy project to carve. If you wish to make the Tramp a little more challenging, just make his head separate and turn it to one side. Adding open eyes would also make this pattern more challenging, but the easily carved, squinted eyes are just as effective on this

figure. The lapel flower was carved separately and attached in the same manner as the butterflies on the Black Face Clown. The Tramp Clown's right hand is resting on the City Dump sign, which is carved separately and doweled to the base on which the figure is standing.

PAINTING NOTES

Tramp Clowns usually appear in dark-colored clothing, with occasional small bright patches or a colorful lapel flower.

CITY
DUMP

Roly Poly Clown

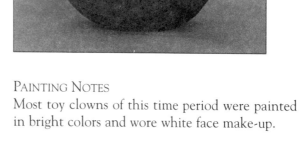

I HAVE BEEN AN ANTIQUE TOY COLLECTOR FOR YEARS, and I find that many toys from the first half of the twentieth century are clowns or have something to do with clowning. The Roly Poly Clown pattern is a replica of a 1910 White Face metal toy.

CARVING TIPS

The Roly Poly Clown may appear to be a bit simple at first to some woodcarvers, but as you begin rounding the body, you may find that it is more difficult than first expected. When carving the body, rotate your work frequently to check for accuracy. The arms and hands, as well as the wrinkles in the collar, are carved with very shallow knife cuts. To carve the head follow the same instructions as for carving the head on the White Face Clown.

PAINTING NOTES

Most toy clowns of this time period were painted in bright colors and wore white face make-up.

THIS VERY INTERESTING PARADE STICK IS PATTERNED after an antique carved around 1900. The original appeared to be shaped entirely with a knife. Its primitive workmanship suggests it may have been carved by a real clown for his personal use. Unusual for a wood carving, this figure was wearing a cloth cape of bright colors with small bells attached.

Parade sticks and musical instruments were among the first clown props ever used. Modern day clowns use such props as giant cameras, midget cars, puppets, ventriloquist dolls and even live pets. Stilt walking and unicycle riding are also popular.

CARVING TIPS
To carve this clown prop a side-view pattern works best. Although the original was carved with only a knife, you may fudge just a little and use a gouge and v-tool when shaping the eyes, ears, and mouth.

To make the cape use the pattern to cut eight pieces of material which will be sewn together side-by-side to form an octagon. Leave the last seam partially open until the cape has been slipped over the painted body. We have added a small black collar and tiny bells as finishing touches on the cape.

I have shortened my parade stick from its original length of 24 inches and mounted it on an attractive base.

PAINTING NOTES
This parade stick is painted in subdued colors to achieve an antique look. This figure represents a court jester from the Middle Ages and wears no facial make-up.

CAPE PATTERN

EVERY YEAR, MY WIFE MARGIE AND I EACH CHOOSE an antique toy from our collection and carve a replica of the toy in miniature size to be used as a Christmas ornament. The little Auguste Clown doll pattern was carved by Margie in 1988, and I carved the jack-in-the-box in 1982. (Only the pattern for the clown is included here.) We enjoy these small figures very much and thought we should include them just for fun.

CARVING TIPS
To make the ornament clown, use a front view pattern when sawing your blank. The woodcarvers knife is the principle tool used for carving this little clown, however, you will want to use the v-tool when shaping the large strands of hair. A 4mm gouge was used to make wrinkles in the collar. The hands and feet have carved seams that have been stitched with an awl to make the clown appear as a stuffed doll.

PAINTING NOTES
The Auguste face is smooth and flat with a round protruding nose. All other facial detail is painted on. After painting the costume, this figure was sprayed with Deft Clear Wood Finish to protect the finish for many years of use as a Christmas ornament.

Clown of the Future

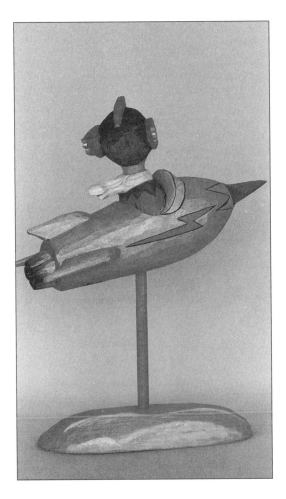

I HAVE ALREADY MENTIONED LOU JACOBS AND what a famous clown he was, but what I did not mention was the act that made him famous. Lou was a contortionist and could fit his six-foot-body into a miniature car he had specially built for his act. The crowd would roar as Lou drove his tiny car around the circus arena and then he would slowly emerge from his little car big feet first.

I'm going to look ahead into the twenty-first century as I create a little Auguste Clown that I call Bobby Blastoff, Clown of the Future. Bobby is also a contortionist and can easily fit himself into his miniature rocketship.

CARVING TIPS

When bandsawing the blank for Bobby's rocketship, use the side-view pattern first. Then draw on and carefully saw the top view. The head is carved separately and turned slightly to the left. Bobby's

flight helmet has characteristics from the 1930s Flash Gordon movie. His rocketship of the future is similar to a toy design from the 1950s.

PAINTING NOTES

Bobby's face has been painted in the traditional Auguste color, and he is wearing a white silk aviator scarf with a red and blue space suit, which has a nine-pointed collar. The rocketship is painted silver with red, yellow and orange trim. Paint the windshield gray and add a few thin streaks of white for reflection. Bobby's support base is painted light blue with a few white fluffy clouds.

I hope you have enjoyed this pattern composed of traditions and ideas from the past used to create an original piece of art called Bobby Blastoff. It is my sincere hope that it will have a creative influence on your wood carving and perhaps turn into a real clown in the future.

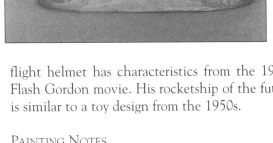

Reference Material

Associations

National Clown Arts Council, Inc.
240 Swimming River Rd.
Colts Neck, NJ 07722
(908) 741-4459

I would like to thank Woodcraft Supply
7845 Emerson Ave.
Parkersburg, WV 26101
for making available the carving tools for the
cover photographs

Museums

Vent Haven Museum, Inc.
235 Chambers Rd.
Walton, KY 41094

Circus World Museum
426 Water Street
Baraboo, WI 53913

Publications

Laugh•Makers Magazine
P.O. Box 160
Syracuse, NY 13215
(315) 492-4523

Don Marcks Circus Report
525 Oak St.
El Cerrito, CA 94530-3699

M-U-M
The Society of American Magicians
7655 John Ave.
St. Louis, MO 63129